RETURN

SIGNAL

Fonograf Editions
Edited by Adie B. Steckel, Jeff Alessandrelli & Ellena Basada
Portland, OR & New York City, NY

Cover and text design by Mike Corrao
Cover art by Cobi Moules

First Edition, First Printing
FONO48

Published by Fonograf Editions
www.fonografeditions.com

Distributed by NYU Press
NYUPress.org

The manufacturer's authorized representative in the EU for product safety is Mare Nostrum Group B.V., Mauritskade 21D, 1091 GC Amsterdam, The Netherlands.
Email: gpsr@mare-nostrum.co.uk.

[clmp]

Fonograf Editions is a proud member of the Community of Literary Magazines and Presses

ISBN: 978-1-964499-76-5
ISBN (ebook): 978-1-964499-81-9

RETURN SIGNAL

TR BRADY

FONOGRAF EDITIONS

CONTENTS

Testosterone Daydream

I was so lonely in the real dream.
I washed all of Lindsey's forks and none of mine.
There was no meal to be had, dream hunger turning
me inside out, dream water running all over the counter.
I am so not rare   there's only an incomplete
number of me. The coin behind my ear,
up my sleeve. The coin I'm referencing
both sides of, the pentacles playing out poorly.

I daydream the real dream, dream Kate holding my shoulders
in the waterless pool, dream James holding my face
in an unfamiliar city. The dream where I'm in love
with each facsimile of me. Where I'm my own
little happy house husband, something that feels gigantic,
a tiny cut in the join of a mouth.

Brittany,

I'm naked in a field. Buried
to my ankles. The grass
high and tan. Some broken blades.
You are sitting on a keg and smoking
and wearing my good shoes.
I ask for a shovel. You give me
two Barbie arms and a stick of gum.
You point to the yellowing sky
then your wrist.

I dig what earth I'm able.
You open the tap.
A siren spreads out under
the cloud bank. Dissonance
in an echo chamber.

It's dark. I'm manning a floodlight.
A girl is car-surfing in a cornfield
and she wants me to see every second.
Little nicotine contrails in her wake.
Another girl is driving the car. She kills
the headlights so it's on me to light their way.

I've never been good at reading minds
and almost lose them in the crop.
The driver makes a sharp turn
at the scarecrow, throwing the other girl
from the roof of the car. She parks behind a shed.

The rustling stops for a while.
When the surfer emerges,
she's alone. She looks to me,
mouths, *did you get that?*
The floodlight dims.
She seems further away than before.

Laying Open

The only way to implicate myself is to admit
the pale blue of the room. The curtains
pulled back. I remove my shirt, my binder,
and hope a neighbor sees my shape.
I google the flight patterns of seagulls
after seeing what I think to be seagulls
flying toward the Iowa River. I think
I might be dying every time I get back
on Zoloft. Dye my hair gray
in preparation. My favorite
pastime, getting gussied and singing
Meredith Brooks' *Bitch* at karaoke and
waxing my eyebrows for the cathartic
experience. My hormones eager
for communion. I hold my chest
and will it do something interesting,
but its magic, gone. A second formation
of gulls, northbound. My search yields little
information. They like to float on an updraft
for as long as possible to conserve
energy. What stilted prayer,
my urge against.

Phantom Mirror

tonight we touch. grandiose
experience, that. my hand,
your hand, your hand, yes,
mine. the mirror
a sort of snare
drum. the field
the bathroom, the players
me. I yearn
the triptych fold in on itself
and leave me out of it.
knock twice for another
image. knock thrice for a better
image. I try to hold
my palm to yours.
the illusion, distance.
the form, other
dimensional.

::

I fear the form of me, the landscape
of whom has been eager with change

time and geography   I must find another

                                          way   to activate

its image, which has the mask of me, but none

of my secrets. I cannot judge their heft
but pinch my hip all the same.

::

still growing, somehow,
            the figure and its quiet architecture.
quick, too   the sacrilege
I keep. trying to work the synth
of me, she extends some limb
or other—the gain,
            high and freckled with impurities,
the source, inscrutable.

it is winter. I must keep
myself made in the good image.
physique being recourse
            for which I have no paragon.

::

the night turns up. i open my window to let it in.
the shower fogged up my bathroom, so i leave
the door open. the night goes in there too.
my red feet. my glow feet. my red hands. my glow
hot. i let the cold night in and let it touch my
warm form. i cannot track the transfer
of energy. i have no tools
to measure the make of me. my mirror,
sweaty. i stick my finger to it.
slide shapes across the surface.
a line. a circle. a curly q. a cute
triangle. emoticon mouth.
icon arrow. # and point past mirror.
to create my shapes, i erase the sheet
of steam. the steam erases itself.
the night pushes past—

Getting By

I had a pill at the wake. I had three beers at the wake.   My socks were wet.
I was on my way to a bar when I got the call and it was raining. It rained for five days.
I had a dry dream every night for five nights.
Your lips chafing mine in all of them. Our red clothes. A fire
in a far-out field. A heat haze silvering a road.
Every time I blinked the fire was closer and   I didn't have enough spit to put it out.
The fields are burning and you're not a pharmacist, but you tuck a little bouquet
of Xanax under my tongue and tell me to save it for later.

I had a pill at your wake   and three beers.
It rained at the funeral and so my socks were wet. The whole time
my mother was straightening my tie. Next to the picture display a little keening
boom box. All your ex-lovers whistling into their bottles. Your mother
straightening your tie.

Testosterone Daydream

At the house party I was a depressed convert. In the inaccurate hour
I take the house apart. A keystroke to a dream. At the house party
I coveted your leather cap and you in it. I had no hereafter
body. Outside, I stood beyond the square of yellow light coming from
inside the house. I mapped my desire for desire. I stray
in the dream of the house party. I take myself apart. Not a good
fight. It was Thursday and fall and I didn't go to the reading,
but I went to the afterparty. I copy paste you to every room.
I try to not notice you. In real time I walk up near you
and change course. I put no clues to you. I wrong myself
to a slight shape and slip out every crack.

Daybreak,

aka exit of darkness, I got your email and wanted to thank you. Iowa City's all ice and snow slush, so I haven't left my apartment for two weeks. my downstairs neighbors are always burning their food and having sex at noon. I went to a party once last fall. I got a new rug from IKEA. my girlfriend and I call our upstairs neighbor *birdman,* even though his name is Benjamin, because he was filling his birdfeeder when we moved in. it's January. fat grey squirrels have claimed the seeds. my weather app says it's 14 below. I'm afraid my car won't ever start again and I'll be stuck in Iowa forever. when I was young in Arkansas a chirping frog kept me up all spring all summer. each chirp longer on the heat waves. this morning is inaudible. little *almost* sounds collecting in the snow outside.

Little Cold Amp

waking into my body my body the bedroom   waking
my body, my body   a bad groom
the groom was tending   no horse   squirrels have taken off
in flurry or fury   the every-third-Wednesday sirens going off I level
my mountain   of laundry   looking for any shirt last night
made holes   in my quilt   frittered   in my fitful   sleep
my chronic leg   buzzes to some sad life   every brink beyond every brink
every nameless   static   wanting to be called   ,yes
each hour hemming   the windows letting   too much in   I redouble
nothing   the dispatch comes   from nowhere

The Sun is a Second Self

The sun cuts across my bedroom.
My compression vest cuts
across my chest, keeps it
not in line but flat.
The sun is a knife, okay?
It's not good at buttering.
My bedroom is not butter
yellow, but too dark
in some places, then far
too bright a slice strikes
across it. I find myself
hot with exposure.
The vivid morning copies
my mouth. A slice turning
in on itself or disappearing.
A slice turning up
or upside down. I flex
my hand but the sun isn't good
at shadow puppets this early.
I make a dog, his perky ear,
his wide waiting mouth.
Nothing to catch or cast onto.
When my pinky cramps
from holding the form
I let the dog go.
I'm practical.
It can't stay. A stratus
moves in. The sun must
be bitter, but I can't

see its shiny edge
or shiny slices. I trace
a line across my breastbone
for a long time.
Enough to learn
the pattern.
Enough to not want
to get used to it.

Testosterone Daydream

I'm a negative twin. A double negative twin. Positively twin!
I dye my hair blonde and look for my twin
but they're gone or a long time ago. A long time ago
my twin was a brunette. I ask my twin to perform
experiments on me but our time is up. I go to sleep and dream
of nothing at all. In the morning my jaw is locked. I massage
my jaw in the shower. The shower casts nothing out of me
even though I ask it to. I shave my jaw to be sharp like my twin.
My twin wears my clothes without asking,
but I don't mind. I tell my twin two truths and one lie,
but my twin doesn't want to play. They're always slipping out
or turning up in the wrong hour. Calling my name from the hall,
washing their hair in my sink, driving my car.
My twin is the exits mysteriously twin.
Here's where they can't be found and I'm lousy about it.
Here's where I look for them in everything.

Fit / fright

eyelids tender from rubbing + reaction   *become irritated once more*
I drive out to Kalona at night   *to see the dark*
+ scream + cry after getting off work at the big box store
When back in Iowa City   *I sit in a BK parking lot to listen to university radio*
+ fret from buyer's   *remorse*

I buy skin cream to prepare myself
for the purpose of trying to be a woman
I apply my chapstick as if primer
not pretty a fortnight in on my mood
stabilizer, I hardly know how many miles
I must drive to see the night
the real night, vast]

last winter I began the sport
of ice-driving, the potential for danger
to see Iowa City
emptily glow w smoke and sodium
vapor from the river
the power plant on the river so monstrous
my first memory of the city
grayscale I crossed the Burlington bridge
by foot and tipped my torso over the railing

just enough to feel
weighty, the rushing of water below
turning, turning [

I was driving my car to keep it warm
in this new cold
in this new cloud
in the world of my breath
long + gray + spreading
spent I spun down a long
hill the amber lights, my shoulders locked
the thrill [

on my days off
on my bright screen
I adjunct + still
consider myself new
to Iowa, my sensibilities not
yet for this flora I am unsteady
in my belief in medicine
in my belief in nature as medicine
I touch my red gums + don't pull
back + I flinch
in my misguided magic [

I pick a psychiatrist who tells me
I'm bipolar +
prescribes 40 dollar fish oil + lamictal
big black box warning looms
heavy w panic I develop
double-vision + rash + blood
shot eyes + a fear of light
+ a first name relationship
w Jackie the telephone nurse
I meet in metered
late one night outside of Mercy

EMERGENCY
HOW COULD I
EMERGE
MY DUSTY VEHICLE
TO THE ROCKY ICE
TO THE MINT
+ BEIGE INTERIOR
OF MERCY SO I
CALL THE COURTESY HOT
LINE + DETAIL
MY BODY FOR HER NOTES
my body for her notes

Name the Fear-Spangled Thing

I go in search of the body,
its buzzed head,
but the glittering grid of its
topography, blinks so unlike mine
            daunting. telepathic
that I am, of course you
would think me capable
of discerning myself
at any juncture, but how
warped the mirror. I desire,
am of desirous nature,
but when imaged
                        a rush
especially in winter
when the trees of Second Ave.,
which I have no name for,
are gussied to some ideal
            and the figure of me
strains to be righted
and simultaneous
and independent
            of its landscape.

Phantom Gender

the ache is lined with ache. the thread,
eventful traction. dawn comes,
a cold cloth. my loss, ever so. the mascara removed, lingers.
how easy my image to overcorrect. I want to show you
a body to some extent
like mine, but she has scrubbed raw and is unfit. for company
I try, but the reach of me minimized. action,
that is I move to strike
my hot cheeks. I tire
in making the contour. the condition:
fractal vanity, what light catches here?

Testosterone Daydream

I think the bar dog smells my sadness.
I feel fondly of his little white socks and
my own electric slippers. Sparks point
fondly from the light switch. The light
switch points fondly to announce the hour.

Let's say an amount of time has passed.
Let's not say which way. Every dog, every
dog. The surprise when a skater rumbles past.

Ask when I dreamed I donned the little socks
and Mary Janes for Liz or turned into a famous twin
in the half-bath. I ask the dog to announce the hour,
but I'm the twin and the dog won't listen to me.
I know he doesn't have to.

Queer Reimagining

after *The Ancient of Days*, by William Blake

I stretch into a starfish, say *big stretch*, when I mean big grief. I try to work my body out, but my body is distracted. I try to work my grief out, but I can't find her. when I can't find my grief I remember my childhood dog. when he yawned my mother would say *big yawn*. I open my mouth to no avail. no glamor. here is a moving image: at the jump I whiffed the ball. here is a still life: the bright ball suspended. I stretch into a star. a blue giant. not strictly defined. many. loosely. my muscles, ablaze. I tire from holding the form of a star. my shoulder's globe everslight. my hand arched at the pinnacle of anything. space occurs in me. I don't want to extend it. it extends.

Imitate / Interface

smearing across yr notice DMs yield pheromones and impulse
gutsy want for to be a damp spot on the floor by yr hand I fluster
I will yr lipstick smear onto my lipstick
I touch my thigh and waxing affection I over
share a dream in which I had a fantasy
held by ghosts posturing as mystics
fraught I mimic their thirst
for ecstasy I commune with my inbox yes I am seeking
adult friendship but won't respond in this fantasy
my morph a hot haunch my crop top unraveling
and then wake thumb to vermilion border
in a swing of sad salty bedclothes stay salty
each cowlick more drastic the tarot says the outlook
sleepless I order glasses with digital block not daylight but blue or other

Testosterone Daydream

I check the analytics for my effective body

I can't sleep from want and wait to be possessed

I buy dumbells and a snowboard and a pair of dress shoes

In the myth, I protect my lips like any man

I hold my tube of chapstick like a child holds a crayon

The amount I remember is horrible in both directions

I record the sound of my voice intermittently for six months

And not again for three years

In that way, I'm practical

What could I resume

Supplication: Early

When Ally and I are in the fifth grade, we ask Mr. and Mrs. Bradley, our Sunday school teachers, to teach us how to tie ties. Mrs. Bradley says it's never too early to start learning, winks at Mr. Bradley. Ally and I both know our verses for the week. The next Sunday they make good, bring a tie for each of us. I'm 11 and always trying to impress Kelly, even though she's not there, and refuse to take the Razorback tie. Kelly's new from Tennessee. I'm a Vols fan for a year.

At home I practice with my dad's burgundy tie, which doubled for Easter and funerals. Wide on right, slim on left. Wide over small, to the left.

Back to school shopping for sixth grade, I'm still too small to shop in the junior's section of Kohl's. I sift through the racks of sequin and graphic tees, when I find a white button up with capped sleeves accompanied by a plaid tie with a big jeweled clip holding together the ends. I'm too excited to wait to wear it on the first day and wear it at open house. Kelly says, why are you wearing a tie, you look ugly, like a boy. Runs off to her new friends, tells everyone I'm an ugly boy. Later that night at the refreshment table, Nick's dad comes over, he's tall and I've been crying. He's close enough I can feel his warmth. He says, you have beautiful eyes. Calls me Twiggy.

I'm reminded of the part of the church service when someone's dad gets up in front of the congregation and apologizes to everyone for cheating on his wife. She's always rigid in the front pew, the preacher's arm around her. After the dad makes his admittance the preacher releases the clip-on mic from his jacket, asks into it if the wife forgives him, holds the mic to her. I can't hear if she nods from where I'm sitting, but the song-leader enters, singing, from the lobby. Everyone's clapping.

The summer before eighth grade Ally's mom, Tasha, a woman close enough to be an aunt, cuts my hair. I show her a picture of Keira Knightley sporting a pixie cut. Tasha and my mother make me promise to always wear makeup. When I do, she pulls my hair back into a loose ponytail, cuts.

I don't wear the tie again for two years. For the first time I'm taller than most of the girls in my grade. All of the football boys in Jr. High dress up for game days. Their father's ties a little too fat. The seams of their shirtsleeves, off the shoulders. It's not a game day, and I'm B-string girl's basketball, but I bring my tie to school in my gym bag. Put it on in a bathroom stall first thing. In science, my last class of the day, Ms. Englert stops the lesson to tell me my tie's too short. That I've done it all wrong.

Phantom Gender: Implied Line

this alien *I wear,*
the sound of which is
disconcertingly alto,
draws attention
from my sternum
to my bald buzzed
head. this way
for tension, *I breathe*
unintentionally flash
my flat crotch
my faint chest.
spectators spread
away from *my frame*
red-raced and confused
I ungender and regender.
my quick character
searches for *some space*
to fasten itself to.

Interlude:

I am not sure this is the sound I was attempting.

Yet I have given myself over to the verve of it.

The rule book is not a rule book, but sheet music.

Notes aside, I cannot see the waves for they are invisible.

As if the theremin of my dreams, when my body leans toward actualization:
what frequency produced what tune?

That is to say, pitch is relative.

But how soon I am to fluster over my instrument. Slim jugular,

the function of which is lost on me.

Be manageable, I tell my glottal, but fry.

Ache as agent. You feel my alto has betrayed you,

but the score has begun.   No side-stepping this discomfort.

Testosterone Daydream

No preparing for my after self,   I summon every copy
giving so much disaster, you   disparate dream mouth,
give me your winnowed hour and I'll give you a lunar trick:
lightbulbs doubling in the window, desire driving
me to doubling and inviting me in. The small us
blowing every fever dream. Newness cropping up
all over the place.   New ants in the tub, new rabbit
in the yard, new cold stint, new symptoms
coming in,   no machine to tell me I'm good.
I imagine   each chord running up against
the next.   Each synapse ringing another.

Morning in Studio with Bread

this morning, the studio cold. the study ongoing, I find myself collecting dull knives. that is, my knives are dulling and I have yet to buy sharp ones or sharpeners. so I saw and saw the bread. and what a hard loaf it is. but not cold. I turn my heat on for the first time. I have no word for my heating unit. it runs along, a mimicry of baseboard. the control knob is turnable, yet no numbers digitize. no crust softens. as if a stranger, my body to my body engendered I am acclimating   am attempting to acclimate.

Touch // Tune

I'm trying to confuse touch for something other than touch. I trace my make
believe chest. The young men next door are whooping around a parking lot
bonfire. My shirt touches all the wrong places so I don't have to. I imagine myself
in my apartment, but with real quiet. It's complicated. I hear everything. The big
bad bass.
The squeaking fan. The other fan, whipping. The whooping young men. The
thrown can
popping. I don't keep count, but the boys punch each other's arms in comradery, throw
each other up against cars, bowing before, like bucks. Bucking.
I unbuckle my belt, undress for the evening. Out of line with the window. My secure
shadow. Bigger than me. Harder lines in harder places. This is proof
of nothing. My body is not a body without
the dissonance of doubt. I'm listening. I'm listening.

Upswing

the actor of my mind   confuses opera   for swing time switch of wicked causation
I sick   put your songs in   me this morning   and collect
aesthetic screensavers of cabins   in the fog   tea lights   millennial pink sweaters
nipple piercings I do want to don   but fear the fraught exhibition
subsequent stick and tug of new hollows I cannot say   I've built a nest
but recognize the floorplan   somewhere excitable   my gambit
in the urge to noise   imagined as music

Can Last

coming down from mania the burn of winter wind picking up my snowbrush
I attempt reach but fragile the point of connection
not extension however the desire to you I try to keep
the good vigil but tire in the loss the urge to find but what
scent in this snowfield what signifier in this sight my accident
is not knowing how much urgency to apply to my risk my tone
my tick I hear you in every sleet a silence magnified tumult

Testosterone Daydream

I become a long-distance runner
I purchase shoes specifically oriented to my job
Of running long distances
At first, I don't make much money
Instead of running away from my problems
I run through them
I run through my dirty kitchen
I run through the checkout line
I run through therapy and don't do my homework
I arrive so many times
In variable conditions
I turn out my pockets and they become ineffective wings

Interlude:

I can tell you   the plants are over
grown   yesterday the neighbor man removed a dead
beaver in our shared alley   a mile east
of the river   the river walk the river runs
here the plants,   heavy with themselves,
posture like this   the beaver,   dead,
was pointing   west   I think it must
have been a beaver   its size said so
after the first day a buzzard   followed by the man
followed by a dark patch of pavement   this morning
I fix my face at the window   the window ac
rattles no aubade   the death bird   not here,   not gone
I could be   heavier with life
I could be a paperweight   I could be a henchman
cutting back the foliage   the excess of green here
it is!   here it is!

Phantom Topography: Implied Line

In spring 2018 my sister texts to say, mom's dad's wife died. I'm in Iowa writing poems and don't go home for the funeral. Not because my mom's dad left her and her three siblings when she was a child and started a new family with the deceased. Not because I'm in retrograde, but really, my image could be better, I guess. I no longer attend funerals.

{ have molted
in zugzwang

More than once my mother referred to her father. I met him when I was in high school. He was broke at the sternum in the big Baptist hospital. Laid up and sewn shut in recovery from a quadruple bypass. My uncle's wife, F., was there and kept saying the nurse looks like a big dyke with that hair a big dyke with that hair a big big dyke with that hair.

{the tackle set for my
trembling mouth – no
taking

When my mom's dad was released from the hospital my mom and our family and her living siblings and their families went to a Father's Day celebration at his church. The pastor called him up to the pulpit and gave him a Father-of-the-Year award, you know the kind of award you get when you cheat certain death and even though you weren't the best father you go up and accept. Then the pastor says something about how my grandfather is a real man and the need from more manly men. Not those Barry Manilow types. Everyone laughs.

{later everyone lays
eyes on my crew cut –

In a tie and sport coat, I was 22 and my first girlfriend, Brittany, was dead and it was her funeral so my mother couldn't say anything about my attire. She'd never seen so many lesbians. It was like when Diane Keaton went to a lesbian bar in *The First Wives Club* to find her lesbian daughter. It was like that in the way that she was shocked even though she knew what she was walking into and there was heavy drinking after. I could list the ways it was nothing like *The First Wives Club*.

Soon / Swoon

half mourning   against my familial quilt   my favorite
blue square   line drawn flowers three rows from the foot
the bed throws of clammy March   my second   Midwest spring
I spend coveting dopamine and rife w/ blue   I levitate
for to reach   things I cannot keep   my image   my ex
doubles as my roommate   says I've been posting thirst
traps I turn pixel pet I've been dreaming   to right
what predicament   pleasure could torque in upswing
pierce my nostril   kill a succulent   how I miss
my sweet   sweet fugue

Testosterone Daydream

The yellow flash of light
The yellow dog I'm becoming

The yellow wasps touching the plants
In front of the window yellow with day

The wall too thick with heavy paint
Swirls pretending to be stucco
A leaf curled in touch against the window

I never count the many veins
I always begin to count the veins

I have no name for this plant
Some baby's breath next to it
Other plants dead or dying
Curl only against themselves

The scratch on the window gives
The impression that the glass is bending

I run my finger over the scratch but do not
Feel it   The sun wobbles its way in

Limitations

forget touching the mirror – forget touching its hands
those floating dead layers – wave reflection
off – groom the personal – ready for the shower
but forget touching the mirror – even if the steam
slicks it – even if you like what you see – what
would your mother think if you left your sweaty
little prints all over the bathroom – forget admiring
the body's flushing cheeks – forget finger painting
forget panting forget dancing forget tracing your red abdomen forget
histrionic flexing – forget touching
the prints of flowers, with their Latin names,
nailed to the stucco – listen, no nailing the body
to relaxation – no toweling the mirror's squeaking
skin – no skinnying the body –no bellying
the plastic curtain – no tuning the showerhead to pressure
wash your hips – no drain digging for the dead's hair,
even if you're standing in a puddle –
even if you like it

Confession

I have a dream in which I mistake the off-ramp for the on-ramp. It's 2:30 in the morning and I'm coming home from a party. I roll all the windows down to stay awake. I want to be able to tell you it was late and I was fine to drive.

It was late.

I only have this dream because the news was on at the gym the night of the accident and I just kept running on the treadmill when the newscaster said which intersection it was.

When I mistake the off-ramp for the on-ramp Little Rock is sleeping and I shouldn't be driving, but I see the DO NOT ENTER sign in time and turn around.

My hands buzzing on the wheel. The night sticky. Quiet. I blame the construction and bad lighting. A month later, when the newscaster says which intersection it is the woman running beside me says something about bad drivers and drugs. I keep running.

Little Rock is dreaming about bad drivers and drugs.

I'm dreaming it's late and I'm coming home from a party. When I take the wrong ramp a fire two cars and a boy.

He pulls you from the car. Does what he can.

I want to be able to tell you it was late and I was fine to drive and the bad lighting and the construction and I didn't hurt anyone I didn't hurt anyone.

Phantom: Adam

I don't want to talk about the body the body talks that body talk
I say I don't want you it doesn't say it wants to begin again
so I hold up my hand mirror my phantom finder

tell me I'm not a body builder ?
tell me I'm not a magic man ?
tell me I'm conceal *I'm telling you*

the body refuses my help I regard my shape shifter, I hardly know
how to divest I can't rest taut seam of sinew and self
how I would unseal

do you want to look at this photo?
It's a rocket about to break it's a hot hot rocket it's a hunk
of metal leaving it's going it's going it's out of here!

I left myself a message on my mirror it was a recipe for a man

I roll out pie dough instead start small use an empty wine
bottle for the rolling pin of course it'll never turn out
my arms tire pricked by sweat and use

I'm telling you this isn't vicious I want to occur
the way memory occurs

Testosterone Daydream

In the dream, my twin and I take clippings from each other.

I have a blister in the shape of an iceberg.

My twin has a separate fishing knife and slices of separate sharp joy.

We trade packets of hormones. My twin says I'll get your back.

No needs kept. No shelled quiet. No cut to the quick.

No not found in nature. Our lucky wants.

Not Pictured

I want to tell you what it looked like   I was in the yard the yard with the truck
stuck in the ruts of its own making   of rain   joy replaced by another
more available feeling   the truck always getting stuck moving branches
to the burn pile   I was scraping up my calves   red lugging limbs
to finish the weekend work   the neighbor's Husky had been downing
chickens for weeks so it's no surprise it eventually got the Maltese
so we had to bury him out back   I was reluctant to eat
from the nearby honeysuckle bush   I was reluctant to eat   that kind of nature
sleepless, I tried to hunt   a locust one night but
just their shells and their shells soundless   I ran around shirtless for long as I could
wanting my image   to be reproduced   in just cargo shorts and sandals
I never swam   in the pond past the pile but when warm
I would lay on the water   warped deck and swirl the oily surface
the hands stretched out on the water were like mine
because of they were   treading

Missouri

Glad, gone. Travelling, also. The quick ornamentation of sidewalks. The dangerous topography of corn-land glowing white with November's hard residue. My second Iowa winter and still without a snowbrush. Every winter I make the drive from Iowa to Arkansas to Iowa. Every drive I attempt to count the rolling hills, but how fast they are to run together.

The rolling hills appear at points to be shifting. I know tectonics must be at some hot slowplay, but not well enough to name the sensation.

Last month, early morning Cedar Rapids, a man and his dog. At first, and again, I couldn't comprehend the scene. The clouds low and flat and grey and the overpasses lower and flatter and greyer. A steady rain. The man in the median wet and screaming. In his arms, a pit bull.

Maybe not the last drive to Arkansas, a deer, nearly dead. Well off the road. At sixty miles an hour I shouldn't have seen it.

The berm off the rock wall, high. The tan grass. Her tan body. But a jerking. But her red mouth.

I tried to imagine her shaking it off, leaping into the forest, but couldn't stomach it. I tried to will a hunter happening upon her. Kept checking my rearview mirror on the long stretch, long past the point I could reasonably see her.

Every drive, after having been driving for a while, I become unsure of my location—the trick of borders being that they are invisible. This drive, no different. Left Iowa's bleached morning early. The indication of Missouri nondescript, save for the fireworks outlet off the highway, which I used to think was in Iowa. Tall and red ribbed metal and open even in the winter.

Nothing like the fireworks stands back home—red and white tents lining Highway 5 every June. Gravel and grass parking and Cave City watermelons and Church of Christ boys.

Suddenly, somewhere, a jake brake, shaking the dog of my daydreams.

Testosterone Daydream

In the negative space, I called your name
You were in a row boat eating jellyfish to survive
I rented a duplex and saved you the other half
I could hear you splashing all night
I could hear my hair growing in the dark
When I was a child my halloween beard garnered compliments
You were at the vanity putting your face on
I tint my windows and drive through many states
I can pretend to know many things
The distance between my navel and my brow
I heard you reading off coordinates
And said yes, that sounds right

March

I have a dream the night is giving us anything but language.

my mother says ---- ---- --- and my partner says - --- ------.

when I'm unable to tell them I don't understand I say - ------ --.

when I wake, tired, I go for a drive. there are a few children

bicycling. a house with great white antlers where a basketball goal should be.

there is a friend I haven't spoken to in nearly a year,

not for lack of love, but notknowinghowness. I don't call him.

my globus comes and grows. my fear perches there, warbles.

I try to catch it, but the sound goes out,

the way all restless things come to go out.

there are no cars out, so I stop at the yield

for maybe minutes. enough time for it to rain and quit raining

or start raining.

Jonathan,

I stole your John Wieners book. I wrote a hard to title poem. I called the poem 'supplication.' the book's cream spine stuck out on my bookshelf where I keep my special rocks I pulled from my back yard and painted a color unnatural. the rocks bookend my hand-me-down records: *The Pretender, Breakfast in America,* other, others. softened yellow of their covers. softened yellow of your fingers. I haven't seen you in years. I leaf through the books I should've given back, a few folded notes to yourself you left between the pages. my oven caught fire last week. this week a sheet of ice shattered my back windshield. I haven't talked to you in since the winter before last, on the phone in the spare room. I said some words. I don't remember

their sound or the taste of their sound. blooming or collapsing.

Testosterone Daydream

I flicked the light. It kept
not coming on. Every feeling
not coming on. The plants
scare in the window.

The window reflects my desk
my little lamp, my stack of books,
and through, the night morning.
The night plants not quite green.

The tea candles, no more
than little plastic cups
now. I'm sure of few things.

I wrote a few things out:
I fell or I found or I howl
or I stole or I float or I flaw

Graveyard in Winter

no, winter. whittle first the atmosphere, the under
current of snow and mirrors of ice. leave my red
hands for last. the frost wants
my tongue to sleep between the rests in this plot,
the agricultural gutter. of land I can say this:
the ground is hard with cold, my figure
is planted in the frozen swale before the gate, the dead
are the only buried that won't rise come spring.
so, what is to fear of a snowy field? a family
grave I was made to visit as a child? my father,
the bearer of every uncle's coffin? the accident
of snow is that when it melts, I'm left
standing where I was. a little stasis ache.

[[Wobble Twilight, River Landing

Not my muscle man, I keep spinning
the creation of spinning
the product of spinning
the byproduct of spinning
ravels along the paved tributary path.
I skate to skim off my estrogen
in the wet summer where everything is edging
forward. I flicker along the stream
which for most of the year is flood or freeze.
the river, the rocks banking the river,
the rocks loved up on by the river,
are sharp and naked and new
as new as rocks can be and actual
and ugly in their unnature. too far down
slope to touch. far from the real hawk
minding her own. the late x transforms to early
y. I am building corporeal.
my sweat stings, my eye says so.
a long coming cloud. the late day transforms
to early night. I pick up my pulse.
the dam churns the rapids out.

Acknowledgments

Thank you to my family, here and gone. Thank you Chandler and Shelby for your enduring support. Thank you Maggie Nipps for sharing this life and the word.

Thank you Brittany Schock, the first butch I knew. The earliest poems here are for you.

Thank you to my undergraduate community at the University of Central Arkansas for their early support and guidance: Stacy Kidd, Sandy Longhorn, Mary Ruth Stewart, John and Stephanie Vanderslice, Mark Lager, Ben Garrett, Jonathan Clark, Addie Rule, Raya Ivy, and Will Dane.

This book would not have been possible without the support of the Iowa Writers' Workshop. Thanks especially to Mark Levine, Elizabeth Willis, James Galvin, Emily Wilson, D.A. Powell, and A.D. Lauren-Abunassar.

Thank you to the friends and writers who sustain me: Miriam Åckervall, Tyler Barreras, Alex Connors, Laur Freymiller, and Jaye Hanselmann-Cox. Thank you Moscow Mountain. Thank you Clay.

Thank you to the editors and readers of the following publications where versions of some of these poems first appeared: *The Adroit Journal, The Arkansas International, Bennington Review, Berkeley Poetry Review, The Boiler, Colorado Review, Copper Nickel, Denver Quarterly, Diagram, Diode, Foundry, Hayden's Ferry Review, Michigan Poetry Review, New Delta Review, New England Review, New South, paperbag, Pinwheel, Pleiades, Poetry Daily, Poetry Northwest, Quarterly West, Salt Hill, The Spectacle, Tin House, The Tiny,* and *Tyger Quarterly.*

I'm especially grateful to everyone at Fonograf Editions. Thank you to Jeff Alessandrelli and Adie B. Steckel. Thank you for believing in and choosing to publish this book. Thank you to Mike Corrao for the beautiful design. Thank you to Cobi Moules for allowing the use of his artwork for the cover.

FONO
GRAF

1. **Eileen Myles**—*Aloha/irish trees* (LP)
2. **Rae Armantrout**—*Conflation* (LP)
3. **Alice Notley**—*Live in Seattle* (LP)
4. **Harmony Holiday**—*The Black Saint and the Sinnerman* (LP)
5. **Susan Howe & Nathaniel Mackey**—*STRAY: A Graphic Tone* (LP)
6. **Annelyse Gelman & Jason Grier**—*About Repulsion* (EP)
7. **Joshua Beckman**—*Some Mechanical Poems To Be Read Aloud* (print)
8. **Dao Strom**—*Instrument/ Traveler's Ode* (print; cassette tape)
9. **Douglas Kearney & Val Jeanty**—*Fodder* (LP)
10. **Mark Leidner**—*Returning the Sword to the Stone* (print)
11. **Charles Valle**—*Proof of Stake: An Elegy* (print)
12. **Emily Kendal Frey**—*LOVABILITY* (print)
13. **Brian Laidlaw and the Family Trade**—*THIS ASTER: adaptations of Emile Nelligan* (LP)
14. **Nathaniel Mackey and The Creaking Breeze Ensemble**—*Fugitive Equation* (compact disc)
15. *FE Magazine* (print)
16. **Brandi Katherine Herrera**—*MOTHER IS A BODY* (print)
17. **Jan Verberkmoes**—*Firewatch* (print)
18. **Krystal Languell**—*Systems Thinking with Flowers* (print)
19. **Matvei Yankelevich**—*Dead Winter* (print)
20. **Cody-Rose Clevidence**—*Dearth & God's Green Mirth* (print)
21. **Hilary Plum**—*Hole Studies* (print)
22. **John Ashbery**—*Live at Sanders Theatre, 1976* (LP)
23. **Alice Notley**—*The Speak Angel Series* (print)
24. **Alice Notley**—*Early Works* (print)
25. **Joshua Marie Wilkinson**—*Trouble Finds You* (print)

26. **Timmy Straw**—*The Thomas Salto* (print)

27. **Audre Lorde**—*At Fassett Studio, 1970* (LP)

28. **Gabriel Palacios**—*A Ten Peso Burial For Which Truth I Sign* (print)

29. **Isabel Zapata, trans. Robin Myers**—*A Whale Is a Country* (print)

30. **Callum Angus**—*Cataract* (print)

31. **Eds. Dao Strom & Jyothi Natarajan**—*A Mouth Holds Many Things: A De-Canon Hybrid-Literary Collection* (print)

32. **Cody-Rose Clevidence**—*The Grimace of Eden, Now* (print)

33. **Jaydra Johnson**—*Low: Notes on Art and Trash* (print)

34. **Jaime Gil de Biedma, trans. James Nolan**—*If Only For a Moment (I'll Never Be Young Again)* (print)

35. **Esther Kondo Heller**—*AR:RANGE:MENTS* (print)

36. **Ahmad Almallah**—*Wrong Winds* (print)

37. **Kimberly Alidio**—*Traceable Relation* (print)

38. **Sara Gilmore**—*The Green Lives* (print)

39. **Darcie Dennigan**—*Little Neck* (print)

40. **Nora Claire Miller**—*Groceries* (print)

41. **Rachel Rahmé**—*Mercurial, or Is That Liberty?* (print)

42. **Eileen Myles**—*Bird Watching and Their First Three Books of Poetry* (print)

43. **Kristen Gleason**—*The Wallet and Other Thefts* (print)

44. **Xuela Zhang**—*To Compare* (print)

45. **Cris Judar, trans. Lara Norgaard**—*They Marched Under the Sun* (print)

46. **Mark Leidner**—*Elegy for Pangaea* (print)

47. **Esteban Rodríguez**—*At the River* (print)

Fonograf Editions is a registered 501(c)(3) nonprofit organization. Find more information about the press at: fonografeditions.com.